PASSWORDS

Also by William Stafford

PASSWORDS

William Stafford

 HarperPerennial

A Division of HarperCollins*Publishers*

Acknowledgments and permissions for previously published materials appear on page 89.

FIRST EDITION

Library of Congress Cataloging-in-Publication Data

Stafford, William, 1914–
    Passwords / William Stafford.—1st ed.
      p.   cm.
    Includes index.
    ISBN 0-06-055293-X
    ISBN 0-06-096587-8 (pbk.)
    I. Title.
    PS3537.T143P34   1991   90-56101
    811'.54—dc20

91 92 93 94 95 MV/FG 10 9 8 7 6 5 4 3 2 1
    93 94 95 **RRD** 10 9 8 7 6 5 4   (pbk.)

Contents

3 COMPARTMENTS OF TRUTH

Dedications
     Pledges
          Commitments

For the past.
For my own path.
For surprises.

For mistakes that worked so well.
For tomorrow if I'm there.
For the next real thing.

Then for carrying it all
through whatever is necessary.
For following the little god who speaks only to me.

Passwords

Might people stumble and wander
for not knowing the right words,
and get lost in their wandering?

So—should you stand in the street
answering all passwords
day and night for any stranger?

You couldn't do that.
But sometimes your words
might link especially to some other person.

Here is a package,
a program of passwords.
It is to bring strangers together.

1　MILEPOSTS

Story Time

Tell that one about Catherine
who carried her doll to college
and when her baby died
she threw her doll in the river.
        Tell that one.

And the one when the old engineer
liked his locomotive so much
he lived there and they had to
build him a house with a whistle.
        I like that.

And the successful racehorse with a fancy stall
fixed up like a Western clubhouse
with an old tennis shoe nailed
for luck above the door.
        That's a good one.

But I'm tired of this long story
where I live, these houses with people
who whisper their real lives away
while eternity runs wild in the street,
        and you suffocate.

Yes, and how about the boy who always
granted others their way to live,
and he gave away his whole life

till at last nothing was left for him?
	Don't tell that one.

Bring me a new one, maybe with a dog
that trots alongside, and a desert with a hidden
river no one else finds, but you go there
and pray and a great voice comes.
	And everything listens.

The Way I Write

In the mornings I lie partly propped up
the way Thomas Jefferson did when he slept
at Monticello. Then I stop and
look away like Emily Dickinson when
she was thinking about the carriage and the fly.

When someone disturbs me I come back
like Pascal from those infinite spaces,
but I don't have his great reassurances
of math following along with me; so somehow
the world around me is even scarier.

Besides, the world on fire of Saint Teresa
surrounds me, and the wild faces Dante
awakened on his descent through those dark
forbidden caverns. But over my roof bends
my own kind sky and the mouse-nibble sound of now.

The sky has waited a long time
for this day. Trees have reached out,
the river has scrambled to get where it is.
And here I bring my little mind
to the edge of the ocean and let it think.

My head lolls to one side as thoughts
pour onto the page, important
additions but immediately obsolete, like waves.

The ocean and I have many pebbles
to find and wash off and roll into shape.

"What happens to all these rocks?" "They
become sand." "And then?" My hand stops.
Thomas Jefferson, Emily Dickinson,
Pascal, Dante—they all pause too.
The sky waits. I lean forward and write.

Reading with Little Sister: A Recollection

The stars have died overhead in their great cold.
Beneath us the sled whispers along. Back there
our mother is gone. They tell us, "If you hold on
the dogs will take you home." And they tell us never
to cry. We'll die too, they say, if we
are ever afraid. All night we hold on.
The stars go down. We are never afraid.

Birthdays

A birthday is when you might not have been born
and you remember the sister you didn't have
because there was a war on. That could have been
you, so it is a happy day and your parents
tell you they are glad. You feel the air
go past. From across the river the sound
of a train comes through the window, and it's
your sister saying good-by to all the years.
Her ghost will be upstairs at bedtime
but you won't tell anybody but will send
your birthday on your breath out into the dark.

The Day Millicent Found the World

Every morning Millicent ventured farther
into the woods. At first she stayed
near light, the edge where bushes grew, where
her way back appeared in glimpses among
dark trunks behind her. Then by farther paths
or openings where giant pines had fallen
she explored ever deeper into
the interior, till one day she stood under a great
dome among columns, the heart of the forest, and knew:
Lost. She had achieved a mysterious world
where any direction would yield only surprise.

And now not only the giant trees were strange
but the ground at her feet had a velvet nearness;
intricate lines on bark wove messages all
around her. Long strokes of golden sunlight
shifted over her feet and hands. She felt
caught up and breathing in a great powerful embrace.
A birdcall wandered forth at leisurely intervals
from an opening on her right: "Come away, Come away."
Never before had she let herself realize
that she was part of the world and that it would follow
wherever she went. She was part of its breath.

Aunt Dolbee called her back that time, a high
voice tapering faintly among the farthest trees,
"Milli-cent! Milli-cent!" And that time she returned,

but slowly, her dress fluttering along pressing
back branches, her feet stirring up the dark smell
of moss, and her face floating forward, a stranger's
face now, with a new depth in it, into the light.

Some Things the World Gave

1

Times in the morning early
when it rained and the long gray
buildings came forward from darkness
offering their windows for light.

2

Evenings out there on the plains
when sunset donated farms
that yearned so far to the west that the world
centered there and bowed down.

3

A teacher at a country school
walking home past a great marsh
where ducks came gliding in—
she saw the boy out hunting and waved.

4

Silence on a hill where the path ended
and then the forest below
moving in one long whisper
as evening touched the leaves.

5

Shelter in winter that day—
a storm coming, but in the lee
of an island in a cover with friends—
oh, little bright cup of sun.

Local Events

A mouth said a bad word. A foot
kicked me. One brick in the pavement
stared into my left eye, and a noise
came close and closer—a siren.

"Listen," someone said, "he asked
for it." Feet shuffled and the sun
went out in a fading glow. A red color
spread slowly across the road.

Then there wasn't any world. No one
was left anywhere, and in the quiet
a long breath shuddered gently out of
something in the road that used to be alive.

Air like the breath from our cellar lifted me
far where the sun was still shining.

News Every Day

Birds don't say it just once. If they like it
they say it again. And again, every morning.
I heard a bird congratulating itself
all day for being a jay.
Nobody cared. But it was glad
all over again, and said so, again.

Many people are fighting each other, in the world.
You could learn that and say, "Many people
are fighting each other, in the world."
It would be true, but saying it wouldn't
make any difference. But you'd say it.
Birds are like that. People are like that.

Faux Pas

Waiting seems to be best. Your remark
balances on edge—maybe no one will notice
when it falls. After a pause, all at the table
shift their attention. You brush crumbs into your hand.

Maybe you will be forgotten. Maybe a tornado
will scatter this day and you will crawl from the wreckage,
knock off the survivors, and emigrate. Years
will pass. Vines will tangle all over this hemisphere.

In the jungle where you live wild animals will snarl at night,
and you will love that sound, so definite: "OK, so I said it."

An Afternoon in the Stacks

Closing the book, I find I have left my head
inside. It is dark in here, but the chapters open
their beautiful spaces and give a rustling sound,
words adjusting themselves to their meaning.
Long passages open at successive pages. An echo,
continuous from the title onward, hums
behind me. From in here the world looms,
a jungle redeemed by these linked sentences
carved out when an author traveled and a reader
kept the way open. When this book ends
I will pull it inside-out like a sock
and throw it back in the library. But the rumor
of it will haunt all that follows in my life.
A candleflame in Tibet leans when I move.

The Origin of *Country*

A child came out on the porch. It was
a soft night, midsummer, stars, a breeze
from the river pressing in and holding
the curtains apart. That night
all out there was an echo.

In the dim light down in the barn cows
waited. The eleven hens roosted on their rafter.
Fireflies made zigzag patterns among the elms.
And a strange glow like a light that would never
go out began to loom for the child there.

From that night sprang the new strain,
a way of permitting night to dwell
over cornfields, a certain delay in sounds
that follow up from the creek. The tradition
of *country* came to that farm.

With a stick in the dust the child
scrawled a design, meaningless,
portentous, not a word, not a circle,
but a figure that the moon silently studied
and passed over and never forgot.

Paso por Aquí

Comanches tell how the buffalo
wore down their own pass through these hills,
herds pouring over for years, not finding
a way but making it by going there.
Comanche myself, I bow my head
in the graveyard at Buffalo Gap and begin
to know the world as a land invented
by breath, its hills and plains guided
and anchored in place by thought, by feet.

Tombstones lean all around—marble, and pitiful
limestone agonies, recording in worn-out words
the travailed, the loved bodies that rest here.
No one comes quietly enough to surprise them;
the earth brims with whatever they gave. It spills
long horizons ahead of us, and we part its grass
from above, staring hard enough to begin
to see a world, long like Texas,
deep as history goes after it happens,
and ahead of us, pawed by our impatience.

We came over the plains. Where are we going?

Old Blue

Some day I'll crank up that Corvette, let it
mumble those marvelous oil-swimming gears
and speak its authority. I'll rock its big wheels
till they roll free onto the drive. Nobody can
stop us then: loaded with everything, we'll pick up
momentum for the hill north of town. Mona,
you didn't value me and it's too late now.
Steve, remember your refusal to go along on
those deals when you all opposed me?—you had
your chance. Good-by, you squealers and grubbies;
good-by, old house that begins to leak, neighbors
gone stodgy, days that lean casually grunting
and snoring together. For anyone who ever needs
the person they slighted, this is my address: "Gone."

Overheard Through an Airduct
in the Reference Library

These cards I sort, I sort by color.
I cannot read; I have no name.
By ignorance, I find what lurks behind the world.

When earthquakes come, the ducks know first.
I cannot read; I have no name.
When someone dies, the dogs can tell.

Between you and life, words form a wall.
I cannot read; I have no name.
These cards I sort, I sort by color.

An Archival Print

God snaps your picture—don't look away—
this room right now, your face tilted
exactly as it is before you can think
or control it. Go ahead, let it betray
all the secret emergencies and still hold
that partial disguise you call your character.

Even your lip, they say, the way it curves
or doesn't, or can't decide, will deliver
bales of evidence. The camera, wide open,
stands ready; the exposure is thirty-five years
or so—after that you have become
whatever the veneer is, all the way through.

Now you want to explain. Your mother
was a certain—how to express it?—*influence.*
Yes. And your father, whatever he was,
you couldn't change that. No. And your town
of course had its limits. Go on, keep talking—
Hold it. Don't move. That's you forever.

2 THE BIG ROOM WHERE THE PLAIN WORLD LIVES

At the Aesthetics Meeting

We invented shape after shape,
color moving to and fro;
then outside where the plain world lives
it began to snow.

The Trouble with Reading

When a goat likes a book, the whole book is gone,
and the meaning has to go find an author again.
But when we read, it's just print—deciphering,
like frost on a window: we learn the meaning
but lose what the frost is, and all that world
pressed so desperately behind.

So some time let's discover how the ink
feels, to be clutching all that eternity onto
page after page. But maybe it is better not
to know; ignorance, that wide country,
rewards you just to accept it. You plunge;
it holds you. And you have become a rich darkness.

Romance

A woman down our street went away and became
the sound of a train on a rainy night,
lingering like a scarf caught in the trees.

To Chicago, some said, but all traces
vanished. Years later a card came—
Valparaiso, but faint, and maybe not her.

Now, whenever it rains, like children
we listen at the window. We know some friends
won't ever come back, really.

But the sound of a train is ours, and Valparaiso.

The Dream of Now

When you wake to the dream of now
from night and its other dream,
you carry day out of the dark
like a flame.

When spring comes north, and flowers
unfold from earth and its even sleep,
you lift summer on with your breath
lest it be lost ever so deep.

Your life you live by the light you find
and follow it on as well as you can,
carrying through darkness wherever you go
your one little fire that will start again.

Atavism

1

Sometimes in the open you look up
where birds go by, or just nothing,
and wait. A dim feeling comes—
you were like this once: there was air,
and quiet; it was by a lake, or
maybe a river—you were alert
as an otter and were suddenly born
like the evening star into wide
still worlds like this one you have found
again, for a moment, in the open.

2

Something is being told in the woods: aisles of
shadow lead away; a branch waves;
a pencil of sunlight slowly travels its
path. A withheld presence almost
speaks, but then retreats, rustles
a patch of brush. You can feel
the centuries ripple—generations
of wandering, discovering, being lost
and found, eating, dying, being born.
A walk through the forest strokes your fur,
the fur you no longer have. And your gaze
down a forest aisle is a strange, long
plunge, dark eyes looking for home.
For delicious minutes you can feel your whiskers
wider than your mind, away out over everything.

Trying to Tell It

The old have a secret.
They can't tell others, for to understand
you have to be old.

You need that soft velvet over your ears
and the blessing of time in your hands.
Any challenging sound has a bell at the end.

The vista you heard on a phone all your life
has moved into your head,
where it lures you to listen away.

The secret is wrapped in a message you begin
to hear even in silence,
and at night it wakes you and calls.

The secret is told to you by touches
that spread a thin layer of understanding
again and again, a hint, another: conviction.

You can't see it or hear it but it's there,
like a live wire, a power inside things,
an art, a fantasy.

You have always wanted more than the earth;
now you have it. You turn to the young.
They do not understand.

Daydreams

1

In my dream of the city, I stride with commuters. We carry
folded newspapers to read. We wait on the curb
and then dodge through traffic. I raise my hand;
a bus stops, and I reach the office in time.
With the others, I talk. We plan what to buy and sell
or where to go next summer on our vacation.

2

In my dream of the factory, others like me, but they see
I am different. Sometimes they question; I hold
the answer in my mind for a while—no one can tell
what I am thinking. I watch the sun find
the next row of workers, and the next, and then the sun
waits while I finish. What I do is all my own.

3

In my dream of Mongolia, I love the grass
and the slight roll of the land. All my life
sings to that little tune of the wind. My shirt
blue, my cap one of those tapestries woven
from musk-ox fur, I herd animals all day,
and at night a balalaika flutters the tent.

The Summer We Didn't Die

That year, that summer, that vacation
we played out there in the cottonwood—
we were young; we had to be brave.
Far out on those limbs above air,

We played out there in the cottonwood
above grown-ups who shouted, "Come down!"
Far out on those limbs above air
we were brave in that summer that year.

Above grown-ups who shouted, "Come down,
you'll be killed!" we were scared but held on.
We were brave in that summer that year.
No one could make us come down.

"You'll be killed!" We were scared, but we held on.
That year, that summer, that vacation,
no one could make us come down.
We were young. We had to be brave.

Remarks on My Character

Waving a flag I retreat a long way beyond
any denial, all the way over the scorched earth,
and come into an arching grove of evasions,
onto those easy paths, one leading to another
and covered ever deeper with shade: I'll never
dare the sun again, that I can promise.

It is time to practice the shrug: "Don't count on
me." Or practice the question that drags its broken
wing over the ground and leads into the swamp
where vines trip anyone in a hurry, and a final
dark pool waits for you to stare at yourself
while shadows move closer over your shoulder.

That's my natural place; I can live where the blurred
faces peer back at me. I like the way
they blend, and no one is ever sure of itself
or likely to settle in unless you scare off
the others. Afraid but so deep no one can follow,
I steal away there, holding my arms like a tree.

You Don't Know the End

Even as you are dying, a part of the world
can be your own—a badger taught me that,
with its foot in a trap on the bank of the Cimarron.

I offered the end of a stick near the lowered head:
space turned into a dream that other things had,
and four long grooves appeared on that hard wood.

My part that day was to learn. It wasn't folklore
I saw, or what anyone said, when I looked
far, past miles around me:

Wherever I went, a new life had begun,
hidden in grass, or waiting beyond the trees.
There is a spirit abiding in everything.

Different Things

1

Steel hardly knows what a hint is, but for thistledown
all you have to do is breathe. And a patch of new cement
will remember a touch forever.

2

One time I asked Agnes to dance. How she
put up her arms—I thought of that this morning
fifty years later.

3

Salmon return out of a wide ocean
and find their home river all the way back
through the bitter current.

4

Under sequoias, tiny blue flowers, dim
all day and almost invisible, grow out of moss.
They reach deep into night for that color.

My Name Is Tillie Olsen

I live by the washing machine. My husband comes home
and calls, "You down there, where's my dinner?"
He sends dirty clothes down the chute, and I call, "Send me
your tired, your poor, your heavily grimed." There's the sound
of the shower, then trampling around, then silence. I stand
thinking like a blowtorch burning our rotten
civilization: "You up there, remember
us workers. I want a new bathing suit and a trip
to Hawaii or Europe—somewhere out of this mess."

During the first spin cycle he comes down eating
bread and peanut butter: "What hath God wrote
today?" He riffles my manuscripts by the ironing board.
"Scribble, scribble. Let's you and me quit my job
and go off to an island," he says. He makes me dizzy:
"Just what I was thinking." He grabs me and we dance
        all through the rinse.

A Key to an Old Farmhouse

One of the raindrops going by
might find that key we lost and wash
it away where it fell from the picnic table
or bounced when we ran. One of the birds
might carry that key to its nest, metal
in the sun, glittering from its deep light
and waiting there, slow. The family then—
swallowed by time—are gone, but that key we lost
shines on, a silver monument that nobody
knows, fumbled by rain, cherished
forever by birds wherever it goes.

Waiting for God

This morning I breathed in. It had rained
early and the sycamore leaves tapped
a few drops that remained, while waving
the air's memory back and forth
over the lawn and into our open
window. Then I breathed out.

This deliberate day eased
past the calendar and waited. Patiently
the sun instructed shadows how to move;
it held them, guided their gradual defining.
In the great quiet I carried my life on,
in again, out again.

3 COMPARTMENTS

OF

TRUTH

The Light by the Barn

The light by the barn that shines all night
pales at dawn when a little breeze comes.

A little breeze comes breathing the fields
from their sleep and waking the slow windmill.

The slow windmill sings the long day
about anguish and loss to the chickens at work.

The little breeze follows the slow windmill
and the chickens at work till the sun goes down—

Then the light by the barn again.

Five A.M.

Still dark, the early morning breathes
a soft sound above the fire. Hooded
lights on porches lead past lawns,
a hedge; I pass the house of the couple
who have the baby, the yard with the little
dog; my feet pad and grit on the pavement, flicker
past streetlights; my arms alternate
easily to my pace. Where are my troubles?

There are people in every country who never
turn into killers, saints have built
sanctuaries on islands and in valleys,
conquerors have quit and gone home, for thousands
of years farmers have worked their fields.
My feet begin the uphill curve
where a thicket spills with birds every spring.
The air doesn't stir. Rain touches my face.

Cover-Up

One thing, don't worry about the mountains;
and some trees, even, might survive, looking
over a shoulder from places too cold for us.

And ahead there, where the lake was, where
we scattered our garbage, the heavy old sludge
will abide for a long, long time.

And some things never told will hide in the deep water:
you know, when the spotlight swings they dive
and will never come out on land.

Climbing Along the River

Willows never forget how it feels
to be young.

Do you remember where you came from?
Gravel remembers.

Even the upper end of the river
believes in the ocean.

Exactly at midnight
yesterday sighs away.

What I believe is,
all animals have one soul.

Over the land they love
they crisscross forever.

Ground Zero

While we slept—
     rain found us last night, easing in
     from the coast, a few leaves at first,
     then ponds. The quietest person in the state
     heard the mild invasion. Before it was over
     every field knew that benediction.

At breakfast—
     while we talked some birds passed, then slanted
     north, wings emphasizing earth's weight
     but overcoming it. "There's no hope,"
     you said. Our table had some flowers
     cascading color from their vase. Newspapers
     muttered repression and shouted revolution.
     A breeze lifted curtains; they waved
     easily. "Why can't someone do something!"
     My hand began its roving, like those curtains,
     and the flowers bending, and the far-off bird wings.

The Gospel Is Whatever Happens

When we say, "Breath,"
a feather starts to fly,
to be itself.
When we talk, truth
is what we mean to say.

A weather vane is
courteous and accurate:
the more it yields,
the more wind lies
where it points the way.

The Eloquent Box

Here is the compartment of truth.
When it opens a light goes on
and shines through the sides, while
all other compartments are locked.

If you tap on this box
you hear something that comes
from your past. You can't tell what
it will be—it will surprise you.

Turn the box over and marvel—
it has worn and smoothed out
since last time. If you hold it still
it begins to hurt your hand.

Now birds come back: a towhee
scratches its note, a blue jay
strikes its blue match across
a bland part of the afternoon.

And the stones that have meaning, they
hold still. Everything waits. Then
the continuing force of being
a stone begins to bear down.

Out through the eloquent box
you stare with your eyes of darkness,
and it is now, and the years have
passed, and it is the world.

Toward the Space Age

We must begin to catch hold of everything
around us, for nobody knows what we
may need. We have to carry along
the air, even; and the weight we once
thought a burden turns out to form
the pulse of our life and the compass for our brain.
Colors balance our fears, and existence
begins to clog unless our thoughts
can occur unwatched and let a fountain of essential silliness
out through our dreams.

And oh I hope we can still arrange
for the wind to blow, and occasionally
some kind of shock to occur, like rain,
and stray adventures no one cares about—
harmless love, immoderate guffaws on corners,
families crawling around the front room growling,
being bears in the piano cave.

Network

It shakes whenever you try—the tree by the door
held lightly, those days that stretch out their soft
gray links to each other, mother and father
bound close and the circle of town
alive when a train struggles past. Desolate,
yes, but connected, everything touches
whatever is left. Nobody ever
escapes, or wants to, really: what reaches
out leads back to the center and shivers
long after you're gone. That's why it's home.

Neighbors

These mountains do their own announcements. They
introduce each other. One at a time
they bow. Some wander away alone
and are never heard from again, though in winter
a cloud pattern pretends to be their snow.

Most mountains have a river and keep
a forest, or even a glacier, off where no one
can follow. I had a mountain once, and even
today—usually in the evening—it breathes
when I do, quiet, a friend beyond the world.

Late, Passing Prairie Farm

All night like a star a single bulb
shines from the eave of the barn.
Light extends itself more and more
feebly into farther angles and overhead
into the trees. Where light ends
the world ends.

Someone left the light burning, but
the farm is alone. There is so much
silence that the house leans toward
the road. The last echo from dust
falling through floor joists happened
years ago.

Owls made a few dark lines across
that glow, but now the light has
erased all but itself—is now a pearl for
birds that move in the dark. They polish
this jewel by air from their wings. This glow
is their still dream.

The sill of the house is worn by
steps of travelers, gone—boards tell
their passage, their ending, copied
into the race. When you pass here, traveler,
you too can't keep from making sounds,
like theirs, that will last.

Signs at Our Place

One chair has this desk across the arm
that swings to let you in, and a writing
pen with tiny "So help me God" etched on the nib.

Over the calendar in the kitchen there's
a reminder that says, no matter the page,
"It is today."

One handle we always pull when we leave,
but we've never known why. It is in the hall,
and says, "This is for everything."

Report from K9 Operator Rover
on the Motel at Grand Island

Four summers ago tar covered a road
near here and was tracked in for a few days
along these halls. Many a cigar burned
itself out at night in puddles of whiskey
spilled over after-shave and powder. When the maid
freshens these rooms every day she sprinkles
a most recent brand of penetrating deodorant
which blends in a life-or-death struggle with
earlier brands. It will be years, and maybe
forever, before the weather can reclaim this place.

Procter & Gamble can fool even a bloodhound; so
I can't tell you the name of the most recent
purification, but it's cheap, it comes in a bottle,
and it smells for years of what pretends to be lemon.
If you smoke, you won't know, but I'm telling you
this invisible mushroom engulfs all that used to be real.

Winnemucca, She

Lived here when eagles owned Stony Mountain
and came in a curve every day screaming
their story: "Tents in the meadow, White Men! White Men!"

Winnemucca, she
calmed the eagles: their holy place
would be preserved in that blue distance
long after mountains forgot our day.

Winnemucca saw
armies march all over our land
like smoke and fire to burn our homes.
And Winnemucca wept. She wept for everyone.

Winnemucca, she
married a Blue Coat, gave him children.
She saved The People, rode hundreds of miles
to bring those armies and The People together in peace.

And the eagles are there.

Cocktail Party Talk

Italic talk. Plain round hand talk.
In a corner fragments of three-dots, dashes,
and exclamations. By the window a face
like a lie detector, turned on while a doll figure
jerks and rambles. The trill of the hostess.
A voice that sounds pink saying, "Eat me."

Poets to Consider for Next Season's Series

Creighton L. Herksheimer the Princeton
    scholar-poet, founder of Scriptism

Filer Wilson the eminent pornographer

Florence Manly the stylish revolutionist

Waylong Cunningsby the well-known upholder
    of critical standards

Rosa Lee Rivers the professional disdainer of stuffiness

Colin Digby the beloved country poet

Cruncher Gaspard the popular street poet
    and reader in taverns

Crispena I. Auker the famous explorer
    of pain

Owl W. Boreson the poet-environmentalist

Amy Vonsky the founder of the Sappho
    Sisterhood

4   ELEGIES

If Only

If only the wind moved, outside, and all else waited,
and at our house nothing moved inside,
and I heard the fumbling air—where could I hide
our pictures and souvenirs, the worn-out
clothes we saved, and letters from all the dead?

Afraid even now, I listen. The lock still holds,
but the first air touches our door where the whispers came.
I roll up my worthless, priceless pack,
turn with one long reverent look,
and go tumbling downwind calling the names.

For a Lost Child

What happens is, the kind of snow that sweeps
Wyoming comes down while I'm asleep. Dawn
finds our sleeping bag but you are gone.
Nowhere now, you call through every storm,
a voice that wanders without a home.

Across bridges that used to find a shore
you pass, and along shadows of trees that fell
before you were born. You are a memory
too strong to leave this world that slips away
even as its precious time goes on.

I glimpse you often, faithful to every country
we ever found, a bright shadow the sun
forgot one day. On a map of Spain
I find your note left from a trip that year
our family traveled: "Daddy, we could meet here."

Going On

On the hollow night a small hand
taps just once. It is our child,
whose eyes reflected me, a tiny mote
but in those eyes a giant man.
A heart beats, and all the world
surges in my breast. Then, the stillest
way a hand can be and still be,
it lies there in mine.

Easy world, you gave it once—
please quietly welcome it back,
that hand.

Consolations

"The broken part heals even stronger than the rest,"
they say. But that takes awhile.
And, "Hurry up," the whole world says.
They tap their feet. And it still hurts on rainy
afternoons when the same absent sun
gives no sign it will ever come back.

"What difference in a hundred years?"
The barn where Agnes hanged her child
will fall by then, and the scrawled words
erase themselves on the floor where rats' feet
run. Boards curl up. Whole new trees
drink what the rivers bring. Things die.

"No good thing is easy." They told us that,
while we dug our fingers into the stones
and looked beseechingly into their eyes.
They say the hurt is good for you. It makes
what comes later a gift all the more
precious in your bleeding hands.

What She Left

The dress with flowers on it and
another dress, only some slipper
shoes, books the kids had given,
part of a letter she was writing. It's
good-by when something stops: the line
of the pen slid over the edge of the paper.
What ever happened to that old picture
she had of the nightingale and the rose?

Four A.M.

Night wears out. Stars that were high go down.
The campfire dies. Shapes from the forest ghost by
so quiet that sleepers on the ground never stir.
Thin under the lid of dawn tomorrow is coming.

Dim floating figures bow to the sleepers
then fade as the light grows. They loom in the dark,
those forest wanderers. They step only in shadows.
For a moment I am one of them, and come awake.

Some night I will breathe out and become
part of the silent forest, floating as they do
toward the thin lids of dawn,
and like them, unknown.

Security

Tomorrow will have an island. Before night
I always find it. Then on to the next island.
These places hidden in the day separate
and come forward if you beckon.
But you have to know they are there before they exist.

Some time there will be a tomorrow without any island.
So far, I haven't let that happen, but after
I'm gone others may become faithless and careless.
Before them will tumble the wide unbroken sea,
and without any hope they will stare at the horizon.

So to you, Friend, I confide my secret:
to be a discoverer you hold close whatever
you find, and after a while you decide
what it is. Then, secure in where you have been,
you turn to the open sea and let go.

Rescue

A fire was burning. In another room
somebody was talking. Sunlight slanted
across the foot of my bed, and a glass of water
gleamed where it waited on a chair near my hand.
I was alive and the pain in my head
was gone. Carefully I tried thinking
of those I had known. I let them walk
and then run, and then open their mouths the way
it used to cause the throbbing. It didn't hurt
anymore. Clearer and clearer I stared
far into the glass. I was cured.

From now on in my life there would be a place
like a scene in a paperweight. One figure in the storm
would be reaching out with my hand for those
who had died. It would always be still in that scene,
no matter what happened. I could come back to it,
carefully, any time, to be saved, and go on.

Long Distance

We didn't know at the time. It was
for us, a telephone call through the world
and nobody answered.

We thought it was a train far off
giving its horn, roving its headlight
side to side in its tunnel of darkness
and shaking the bridge and our house
till dishes rattled, and going away.

We thought it a breath climbing the well where Kim
almost fell in; it was a breath saying his name,
and "Almost got you," but we piled boards
and bricks on top and held off that voice.

Or maybe it was the song in the stove—
walnut and elm giving forth stored sunlight
through that narrow glass eye on the front
in the black door that held in the fire.

Or a sigh from under the mound of snow where Bret's
little car with its toy wheels nestled all winter
ready to roll, come spring, and varoom
when his feet toddled it along.

Or—listen—in the cardboard house
we built by the kitchen wall, a doorknob

drawn with crayon, Kit's little window peeking
out by the table—is it a message from there?

And from Aunt Helen's room where she sews
all day on a comforter made out of pieces of Grandma's
dresses, and the suits for church—maybe those
patches rustle their message in her fingers:
"Dorothy, for you, and for all the family I sew
that we may be warm in the house by the tracks."

I don't know, but there was a voice,
those times, a call through the world that almost
rang everywhere, and we looked up—Dorothy, Helen,
Bret, Kim, Kit—and only the snow
shifted its foot outside in the wind,
and nobody heard.

Disposal

Paste her picture back of the mirror
and close it. Let landscape be
the focus of whatever the next scene is—
that's a face you can try to forget, and the weather
visits often this time of year.

You can throw her furniture out. Let the rain
decide what to keep and what to dissolve
or slash into bits, a ritual forgetting
that the world makes happen in its own way
from this time on, outside or in.

Now slowly release her name. It spins
miles long like a thread along the wind.

Your Life

You will walk toward the mirror,
closer and closer, then flow
into the glass. You will disappear
some day like that, being
more real, more true, at the last.

You learn what you are, but slowly,
a child, a woman, a man,
a self often shattered, and pieces
put together again till the end:
you halt, the glass opens—

A surface, an image, a past.

Yes

It could happen any time, tornado,
earthquake, Armageddon. It could happen.
Or sunshine, love, salvation.

It could, you know. That's why we wake
and look out—no guarantees
in this life.

But some bonuses, like morning,
like right now, like noon,
like evening.

Listening Around

Any Breeze to Willow:
    "You like to dance?"
Willow to Any Breeze:
    "Yes, oh yes."

Oak to Roots:
    "Think we can live?"
Roots to Oak:
    "Positive."

Dandelion Blossom:
    "When you're ready, say."
Dandelion Seed:
    "OK. OK."

Summer to Autumn:
    "Who carries my message to snow?"
Butterfly on a blossom:
    "When it's time, I'll go."

All to each other:
    "What to say to strong wind?"
Each other to All:
    "Be mine, Dear Friend."

5 VITA

What's in My Journal

Odd things, like a button drawer. Mean
things, fishhooks, barbs in your hand.
But marbles too. A genius for being agreeable.
Junkyard crucifixes, voluptuous
discards. Space for knickknacks, and for
Alaska. Evidence to hang me, or to beatify.
Clues that lead nowhere, that never connected
anyway. Deliberate obfuscation, the kind
that takes genius. Chasms in character.
Loud omissions. Mornings that yawn above
a new grave. Pages you know exist
but you can't find them. Someone's terribly
inevitable life story, maybe mine.

Evolution

The thing is, I'm still
an animal. What is a spirit,
I wonder. But I only wonder:
I'll never know.

Night comes and I'm hungry.
Tempted by anything, or called
by my peculiar appetites,
I turn aside, faithfully.

What comes before me
transforms into my life.
"Truth," I say, and it answers,
"I'm what you need."

I sing, and a song shaped like a bird
flies out of my mouth.

Merci Beaucoup

It would help if no one ever mentioned
France again. Its words are the ones
that get me most into trouble, especially
naïve and *folie*. Someone sits down
beside me in church and says, "Bonjour."
"Likewise," I say, and they look at me.
See what I mean? It's a French look, and I never
get used to that other word they begin to think of.

Or my lady friend says, "Merci," and right away
I'm caught up in France, wanting to say adiós
but usually saying, "Likewise," as nice as I can
so that she'll see I'm agreeable, no matter
what language we're in. But I can tell she's thinking,
"Far out," the way they say it over there.

Here's the thing—it's not the words, really;
it's being lost from that high ground you have
if you're the one who's the insider. It's the "Mother"
tongue that says, "Be the way I tell you
and you can have my approval but don't ask any questions."
So I don't. I'm back home at the foot of the table
holding the fork right, learning to say, "Likewise."

Young

Before time had a name, when win
or lose were the same, in a forsaken
town I lived unnoticed, blessed.
Remember when shadows played
because there were leaves in the wind?
And people came to our door from a land
where stories were real?
Barefoot, we traveled the roads
all summer. At night we drew pictures
of home with smoke from the chimney.
And we frowned when we read,
so we could understand.

After the years came true, but before
their cost, I played in that big world, too,
and often won: this face was known;
gold came into these hands.
But unwieldy hours overwhelmed
my time. All I intended blew away.
The best of my roads went wrong,
no matter my age, no matter
how long I tried.
It was far, it was dim,
toward the last. And nobody knew how
heavy it was by the end,
for that same being who lived back then.

Don't you see how it was, for a child?
Don't you understand?

It's All Right

Someone you trusted has treated you bad.
Someone has used you to vent their ill temper.
Did you expect anything different?
Your work—better than some others'—has languished,
neglected. Or a job you tried was too hard,
and you failed. Maybe weather or bad luck
spoiled what you did. That grudge, held against you
for years after you patched up, has flared,
and you've lost a friend for a time. Things
at home aren't so good; on the job your spirits
have sunk. But just when the worst bears down
you find a pretty bubble in your soup at noon,
and outside at work a bird says, "Hi!"
Slowly the sun creeps along the floor;
it is coming your way. It touches your shoe.

Life Work

Even now in my hands the feel of the shovel comes back,
the shock of gravel or sand. Sun-scorch on my shoulders
bears down. The boss is walking around barking.
All the cement mixers rattle and jolt.

That day the trench we are digging goes deeper
and deeper, over my head; then the earth heaves
in one giant coffin gulp. They keep
digging and pulling and haul me out still breathing.

The sky, right there, was a precious cobalt dome
so near it pressed on my face. Beside me my hands
lay twitching and begging at the end of my arms.
Nothing is far anymore, after that trench, the stones. . . .

Oh near, and blessing again and again: my breath.
And the sky, and steady against my back, the earth.

In Camp

That winter of the war, every day
sprang outward. I was a prisoner.
Someone brought me gifts. That year
now is far: birds can't fly
the miles to find a forgotten cause.

No task I do today has justice
at the end. All I know is
my degree of leaning in this wind
where—once the mind springs free—
every cause has reason
but reason has no law.

In camps like that, if I should go again,
I'd still study the gospel and play the accordion.

How These Words Happened

In winter, in the dark hours, when others
were asleep, I found these words and put them
together by their appetites and respect for
each other. In stillness, they jostled. They traded
meanings while pretending to have only one.

Monstrous alliances never dreamed of before
began. Sometimes they last. Never again
do they separate in this world. They die
together. They have a fidelity that no
purpose or pretense can ever break.

And all of this happens like magic to the words
in those dark hours when others sleep.

Some Words in Place of a Wailing Wall

The people you choose are the chosen people.

Saplings by the river have to grow
from stones. Near the bridge in freezing
dawnlight you can hear the duck with the injured
wing. Lost from each other and panicked
by a wind from winter, the killdeer zigzag
over sandbars, calling and calling.

When you think about it, we were lucky,
though our fields blew away in dust. We had
a house, and every morning we could shake
dust off our beds and hurry over frozen
floors to the stove we kept stoked with corncobs.

Our neighbors the Talbots were friends, the only black
farmers near town; and we could go help
call their cows in with their pretty names.
The woman had a soft voice. I can still hear it.

Agnes, our school beauty, sang in a rock
band. She can't hear anymore.
Doug, the class president, fought overseas.
He was a hero and made lots of friends
with money, and he got some. He's dead.

If you survive you can tell about things:
the sky that never made any promises anyway,
and our tornado that made enough instant

rubble to last the rest of your life.
Those who complain, they are alive.

The last time I went home I walked
over the bridge and listened, and stood
by the pasture where the woman lived
with the soft voice, where she died.

Something to Declare

They have never had a war big enough
to slow that pulse in the earth under
our path near that old river.

Even as a swallow swims through the air
a certain day skips and returns, hungry for
the feel and lift of the time passed by.

That was the place where I lived awhile
dragging a wing, and the spin of the world
started its tilt into where it is now.

They say that history is going on somewhere.
They say it won't stop. I have held
one picture still for a long time and waited.

This is only a little report floated
into the slow current so the wind will know
which way to come if it wants to find me.

The Size of a Fist

This engine started years ago—many—,
small heart pounding, lungs gasping,
reaching for air, fist curled and ready,
all those months and the subtle tides: nursery,
the schoolground terror, engine beat-beat,
work in the fields, hoe, shovel, wheelbarrow,
engine steady, then on through rooms, faces
grim, turned aside often, beat, move on,
beat, late at night, where? where rest?
even today—who is this old guy?—,
beat, beat, engine cruising, day, night,
beat and away.

Bonuses

Any island, or a break in the weather,
or resting awhile under
bridges or by a rock in the sun—
these offer themselves.
You know these intervals allowed,
moment by moment, lost
in the large parade of the days.

Even a hesitation while a door
opens can balloon
and then there's an arch with
all you need, sheltered there.
All through your life.
Island by island.

Vita

God guided my hand
and it wrote,
"Forget my name."

World, please note—
a life went by, just
a life, no claims,

A stutter in the millions
of stars that pass,
a voice that lulled—

A glance
and a world
and a hand.

Grateful acknowledgment to the following publications and institutions, where some of these poems first appeared: *Agni Review:* "Vita"; *America:* "Five A.M."; *The And Review:* "News Every Day," "Some Words in Place of a Wailing Wall"; *Antaeus:* "Something to Declare"; *Artful Dodge:* "Cover-Up," "Waiting for God"; *Bristlecone:* "Neighbors"; *Calapooya Collage:* "Faux Pas," "Romance"; *Caliban:* "Local Events"; *Chariton Review:* "You Don't Know the End"; *Clockwatch Review:* "Different Things"; *Cornell Review:* "What She Left"; *Country Journal:* "Listening Around"; *Crosscurrents:* "Birthdays"; *Cutbank:* "It's All Right"; *Farmer's Market:* "The Light by the Barn"; *Field:* "An Archival Print," "Evolution," "For a Lost Child," "Ground Zero," "Story Time," "The Trouble with Reading," "What's in My Journal"; *5 A.M.:* "How These Words Happened"; *Fort Valley State College Journal:* "An Afternoon in the Stacks"; *The Georgia Review:* "Remarks on My Character"; *The Green Mountain Review:* "Report from K9 Operator Rover on the Motel at Grand Island"; *Hawaii Review:* "Security"; *Innisfree:* "Overheard Through an Airduct in the Reference Library"; *The Iowa Review:* "Some Things the World Gave"; *Jeopardy:* "Cocktail Party Talk"; *Limberlost Press:* "Climbing Along the River"; *Literary Olympics II:* "Disposal"; *Long Pond Review:* "Atavism"; *Main Street Press:* "Late, Passing Prairie Farm"; *Milkweed Chronicle:* "The Dream of Now"; *MSS:* "Reading with Little Sister: A Recollection"; *The Nation:* "Going On"; *Negative Capability:* "The Summer We Didn't Die"; *New Letters:* "If Only," "The Size of a Fist," "Winnemucca, She"; *Northwest Review:* "In Camp"; *Occident:* "My Name Is Tillie Olsen," "Poets to Consider for Next Season's Series"; *Panoply:* "Young"; *Poetry:* "The Day Millicent Found the World," "Your Life"; *Poetry Kanto:* "Daydreams"; *Poetry Northwest:* "Long Distance"; *Sea Pen Press:* "Passwords"; *Sequoia:* "Yes"; *Sidewinder:* "Paso por Aquí"; *The Small Farm:* "The Eloquent Box"; "A Key to an Old Farmhouse," "Rescue"; *Spectrum:* "Old Blue"; *Stoney Lonesome:* "The Gospel Is Whatever Happens"; *Tendril:* "Network"; *Virginia Quarterly Review:* "The Way I Write," "Consolations"; *The Voyageur:* "Toward the Space Age"; *Western Humanities Review:* "At the Aesthetics Meeting"; *Willamette Journal of the Liberal Arts:* "Trying to Tell It"; *Willawaw:* "Merci Beaucoup"; *The Wooster Review:* "Life Work," "The Origin of *Country*"; *Yankee:* "Signs at Our Place."

"Bonuses" first appeared in the *Cimarron Review* and is reprinted here with the permission of the Board of Regents for Oklahoma State University, holders of the copyright.

Index of Titles

ABOUT THE AUTHOR

William Stafford was born in Hutchinson, Kansas, in 1914. He has won not only the National Book Award but also the Award in Literature of the American Academy and Institute of Arts and Letters and the Shelley Memorial Award. He has served as Consultant in Poetry for the Library of Congress and on the Literature Commission of the National Council of Teachers of English, and he has lectured widely for the U.S. Information Service in Egypt, India, Pakistan, Iran, Nepal, Bangladesh, Singapore, and Thailand. He lives in Lake Oswego, Oregon.